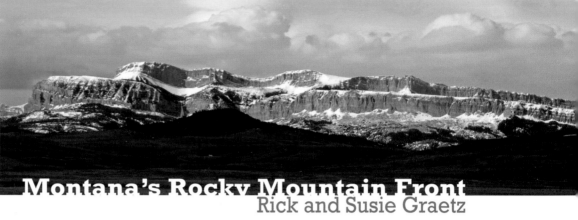

Montana's Rocky Mountain Front

Rick and Susie Graetz

A presence,

a treasure,

and one of the

most spectacular

120 miles

of geography

on the continent.

Above: Wall of the Rocky Mountain Front.

Photo: TARA CLARK

Cover: Near Pishkun Reservoir, southwest of Choteau.

Photo: JOHN LAMBING

Montana's Rocky Mountain Front

©2016 Northern Rockies Publishing

Rick and Susie Graetz

Box 161656

Big Sky, Montana 59716

Published by

NORTHERN ROCKIES PUBLISHING

and the University of Montana Press

All color, design, editing and prepress work done in
Montana, USA

Design: Designworks | Graphic Design, Kalispell, MT

Prepress: Digital Planet, Kalispell, MT

Printed in Korea

Right: Purple lupine, pink
fuzzy-tongue penstemon, and
white miner's candle weave a
colorful pattern across the prairie.

Photo: DOUGLASS DYE

Where the prairie

meets the

mountains…

no transition zone

of slowly rising

foothills here.

Just the ever-flowing

land waves of the

Great Plains

crashing up against

the naked heights

of the Front's

fortress-like reefs.

Crown Mountain area of the Rocky
Mountain Front.

Photo: JEFF VAN TINE

MONTANA'S ROCKY MOUNTAIN FRONT

by Rick and Susie Graetz

It is here, along "the Front" that the Great Plains skids to an abrupt halt against the escarpment of the Rockies.

It's a journey we've made countless times over the decades, always looking forward to another opportunity. Just beyond the hamlet of Wolf Creek, Montana quiet US Hwy 287 points north leading through short grass prairie and sprawling ranch lands. Reaching the Dearborn River crossing, the road gradually climbs a long rise. Topping out, instantly it is in front of you—all at once. Seemingly stretching forever northward is a grand piece of American geography... Montana's Rocky Mountain Front.

Beyond the reach of recorded history, ancient peoples migrating from inner Asia crossed into North America by way of a land bridge spanning an area now occupied by the Bering Sea. They then trekked through the Yukon River Valley of Alaska before journeying south through Canada, Montana and beyond. Their guiding marker was the eastern rim of a

daunting, natural barrier, this same Rocky Mountain Front we marvel at today. The passage they established is now known as the Great North Trail.

Here, along "the Front," the Great Plains skids to an abrupt halt hard up against the soaring escarpment of the Northern Rockies. No transition zone of slowly rising foothills; the mountain wall wastes no space in making its existence felt. And what a colossal presence, fortress-like reefs ascending to naked heights two to four thousand feet above their base!

Looking toward the sunrise from the Rocky Mountain Front, the horizon, a soothing fusion of earth and sky, appears endless. This is the landscape's softer, gentler side. Short-lived hills intersperse with buttes, river bottoms, prairie pot holes, flatland, clusters of fens, and stands of deciduous and conifer trees. It's this contrast of simple grandeur and the explosive power of the mountains that has inspired people to love and cherish this most uncommon place.

The Rocky Mountain Front stretches 152 miles from Hwy 2 in the north to Hwy 200 on its southern end.

Photo: JEFF VAN TINE

As portrayed in this essay, the Rocky Mountain Front covers a 152-mile span of ground from US Hwy 2 in the north at Browning to Montana Hwy 200 in the south. It is also a guardian of the Bob Marshall Wilderness complex and a key component of the Crown of the Continent ecosystem. Its trails lead to some of the most diverse wilderness in America, and its canyons serve as passageways for migrating wildlife. Everything that this place has to offer ranks it as one of the planet's most magnificent treasures.

Water is the essence of any natural system, and the RMF is long on streams, creeks, and rivers. Born from springs, snowmelt, and ice accumulated in caves, water pouring from the high country forms the Dearborn, Sun, and Two Medicine rivers; South, North, and West forks of the Teton River; and both Birch and Badger creeks—all fabled waterways, which add immensely to the beauty and aura of this environment.

And then there are the wild creatures that claim this storied land. History proves that the area's environmental and economic health depends on the well being of its wildlife. And today, the Front is indeed alive and rich with fauna.

Native American tribes relied on the Front's extensive game populations far back into pre-history. Wildlife sustained both their physical and spiritual lives, and Indian spirituality emphasizes the sacredness of wild places. Traditionalists still journey on vision quests and seek personal animal spirit guides just as their ancestors did. Badger Creek, Goat Mountain, Elk Pass, and Antelope Butte—such places stress the importance of wildlife and sanctity along the RMF to indigenous peoples.

From a natural perspective, this rich gathering of wildlife is owing to an elevational and climatic gradient—an ecotone—on the landscape. Here is a spectacular geographic transition of landscapes rising from riparian areas to short grass prairie and upward to shrubs, open forests, precipitous cliffs and lofty summits, providing living space for 43 mammals and 110 species of birds.

Good conservation practices equal a healthy deer population on the Front.

Photo: TONY BYNUM

The Rocky Mountain Front is home to the last Plains grizzlies in the world. In March, the males leave their mountain dens and migrate to lower elevations to forage. In late April, sometimes early May, females with their cubs of the year move into the lower reaches. Fingers of wetlands or fens, as they are best known, are where these giant bears still venture to the prairie they roamed when Lewis and Clark explored Montana. Use of their former range is increasing (it's the only place in the lower 48 states where this is occurring). At 16,000 acres, Pine Butte Swamp Preserve, an extensive peat-land fed by mineral-rich groundwater, is the largest of these wetland complexes used by these charismatic bears.

Amongst some other wild creatures that call the Front home are the elusive wolverines, as well as one of the largest native bighorn sheep and goat populations in the nation. Gray wolves again frequent the Front's northern canyons, and jagged reefs, and soaring walls provide sanctuary for golden eagles and prairie and peregrine falcons. The southern reaches serve as wintering ground for the second largest migratory elk herd in the nation as well as deer and antelope.

And interestingly enough, shimmering west slope cutthroat trout, for the most part found only west of the Continental Divide, find some of the streams of the region to be to their liking. It can be said that with the exception of bison, every wild species that was here when the Corps of Discovery came up the Missouri in 1805 is in residence!

And there is another special bit of RMF habitat. In mid-March, reminiscent of a day at the world's busiest airport, an unbelievable 10,000 tundra swans, as many as 300,000 snow geese, and thousands of other species begin arriving on the Freezeout Lake Wildlife Management Area outside of Fairfield. Squadrons of Concordes (tundra swans) and convoys of 747s (snow geese) circle with military precision above the wetland waiting their turn to land. Fueling up each morning and evening in the nearby grain fields, the sated airliners then spend their days loudly conversing and resting on the lake. Within two weeks time, they will have straightened out their itineraries and departed for various points north.

In mid-March, Freezeout Lake becomes "Woodstock" for waterfowl.

Photo: RICK and SUSIE GRAETZ

Indeed, the area's conservation history is rooted in its natural critters.

During a dark period in Montana's history, wildlife on the Front was imperiled from overhunting by the whites, diseases introduced by cattle, and the lack of protected winter range outside of the mountains. In 1907, the Great Falls Tribune estimated there to be a mere 300 elk left in the Sun River country. They declared the fact that deer were but a "remnant" and claimed bighorn sheep "too few to count."

The great Granville Stuart attempted to explain the rapid change that occurred in two short years when he wrote, "In 1880 the country was practically uninhabited (by people). Thousands of buffalo darkened the rolling plains. There were deer, antelope, elk, wolves, and coyotes on every hill and in every ravine and thicket... by the fall of 1883 there was not one buffalo remaining on the range and the antelope, elk, and deer were indeed scarce."

In 1941, Forest Ranger Ellers Koch wrote, "the South Fork of the Flathead and the Sun River country is today considered excellent game country. Deer, elk, and goats are relatively abundant. Yet in the fall of 1905 and again in 1906, I rode for a month with a pack outfit to the wildest part of that country with a rifle and on my saddle, and with the exception of one goat, I never saw or got a shot at a single big game animal."

The virtual disappearance of wildlife from the Front and the eastern Bob Marshall did not go unnoticed. Alarmed, by 1910, folks from all political persuasions and interest groups rose up and came together to find a solution. Realizing wildlife needed sheltered habitat to thrive, the state's first wildlife reserve, the Sun River Game Preserve, came into being in 1913. Since then, this legacy of conservation has passed from generation to generation. Over time, more havens were created. The Sun River, the Blackleaf, and the Ear Mountain wildlife management areas are all under the care of Montana Fish, Wildlife and Parks, and The Nature Conservancy of Montana oversees the Pine Butte Swamp Preserve.

Ellers Koch,
US Forest Service
Ranger 1903-1943.

Photo:
US FOREST SERVICE

The Rocky Mountain Front is home to one of the nation's largest native bighorn sheep populations.

"I doubt the practical sense of claiming kinship to a mountain, but sometimes it seems to me that Ear Mountain and I are on a common journey, made relatives by times and vicissitudes. Of course, its life will outlast mine, but I'd rather it missed me than I grieved for it.

I'm not alone in my feelings for what was originally called Elephant Ear Butte. Neighbors share my sentiments and look often to it for reassurance in their unassured lives."

—A. B. Guthrie, Jr. 1901-1991

Ear Mountain.

Photo: TONY BYNUM

Many ranchers have put their land into conservation easements.

In 2006, Montanans successfully worked with their two Senators to pass legislation stopping new federal oil and gas leasing on the Front. This allows existing leases to be retired after they are voluntarily donated or sold, ensuring that critical wildlife habitat and public access are protected. In the last eight years under this provision, over 100,000 acres along the Front with valid gas and oil leases have been permanently retired. In December 2014, the US Congress passed the RMF Heritage Act. This added 67,000 acres to the Bob Marshall and Scapegoat Wilderness Areas and designated other federal lands on the Front as "Conservation Management Areas."

The Rocky Mountain Front, however, is more than just a collection of scenic splendor and a wild animal haven. Though we humans are part of the system, our imprint is minimal and for the most part confined to a handful of small, well-spaced communities and a scattering of multi-generational ranches. The towns, set well to the east of the mountains, are unobtrusive. Strung out along 152 miles of a two-lane highway, they are the pleasant communities of Augusta, Choteau, Fairfield, Bynum, Pendroy, Dupuyer, Heart Butte, Browning and East Glacier, with a total population under 5,000 folks. With the exception of Browning, all rely on ranching, outfitting, and some farming to sustain their economies. Browning is the base for the Blackfeet Reservation and hence tribal government is a large employer.

Ranching dominates the agricultural sector. The fact that these cow-calf operations have been sustainable for so long provides a key to the pristine nature of this piece of Montana. Many ranchers have put their land into conservation easements—more than 200,000 acres as of this writing—with The Nature Conservancy and the US Fish and Wildlife Service playing the largest roles. Other organizations such as the Montana Land Reliance and Montana Fish, Wildlife and Parks are also involved in the easement process.

Before the European invasion of Montana, the first stewards of this expanse of prairie-meets-mountains were the many native peoples who relied on the land and its bison herds for their food supply. The last group to occupy and consider it their realm was the Blackfeet Nation. They left behind, for the most part, only footprints and trails. Today, the most recent of the original owners reside on the Blackfeet Reservation in the northern sector of the Rocky Mountain Front. A concerted effort is being made to preserve traditions, including their language, and to buy back land that had previously been bought by non-tribal members.

Ranchers are the mainstay of the Front's economy.

Photo: JEFF VAN TINE

American Indian Days celebrates Blackfeet tribal traditions.

Photo: RICK and SUSIE GRAETZ

In 1973, the Badger-Two Medicine area was declared "sacred ground" by the Blackfeet Tribal Council.

The northern 130,000 acres of the Front adjacent to the reservation are known as the Badger-Two Medicine area, which in 1973 was declared "sacred ground" by the Blackfeet Tribal Council, as it is the focus of their creation stories. The area has recently been recognized as a Traditional Cultural District under the National Historic Preservation Act because of its religious and cultural significance to the Blackfeet people.

Abundant and diverse wildlife populations place the Front in the top one percent of the best wildlife habitat in the United States. In terms of biodiversity, it is unmatched. These are just two of the reasons the tribe has been instrumental in the fight to keep the Rocky Mountain Front free of development.

The meadowlark, Montana's State Bird

Photo: JEFF VAN TINE

Fens provide spring and summer feeding grounds for sow grizzly bears with cubs.

Photo: DAVE HANNA

Building and Shaping the Rocky Mountain Front

Intrinsic to the Front's commanding physical presence are the myriad forces that formed it: floods, faulting, upheavals, glaciers, winds, and volcanic activity: natural influences and the work of ice at its best!

While mountains were being built to the west, sand, silt, and mud were being deposited on the floor of a shallow inland sea that once covered the northern prairie. As the water receded, the sediments lithified into the shale, mudstone, siltstone, and the sandstone surface we now see.

From the air, looking west from the face of the Front to the Continental Divide and the Chinese Wall, a 20-mile-wide swath of lengthy north-south trending mountain ridges dominates. This overthrust geology was created by an intense compression deep within the earth that broke thick, elongated rock layers, which were then lifted and forced into a slanted position and shoved eastward anywhere from 30-50 miles over the younger prairie foundation. Typical of overthrusting, the western exposures slope gradually downward, while the eastern aspects are precipitous.

Wetlands near Dupuyer Creek.

Photo: JEFF VAN TINE

The crests of each rise are of erosion resistant material, but the underlying strata of the lower reaches wear away more easily, hence, in between, deep narrow valleys formed. One of the best places to observe at least four of the overthrust formations is from the Sun River Canyon road west of Augusta. Sedimentary rocks—gray Madison limestone—dominate the core and surface of the Rocky Mountain Front.

While drab in color, they are filled with many fossils, including shellfish remnants, indicating their long ago underwater existence. Other fossils include coral that look like honeycombs

embedded in rock and blue-green algae, the first known form of life in these parts. Limestone ($CaCO_3$) is a mineralized form of calcite; hence, acid in rainwater and snowmelt act on it, forming wild etchings, rough surfaces, and mysterious caves. Jefferson dolomite is another sedimentary rock found in the walls of the Front. Generally dark brown or black, it has a malodorous scent when freshly broken. Abundant organic matter trapped in the rock causes both the dark color and the foul smell.

Below Castle Reef, the Sun River flows out to the prairie.

Photo: JOHN LAMBING

Volcanic processes also contributed to the uniqueness of this landscape. Haystack Butte, a distinct conical landmark southwest of Augusta, protrudes a bit east of the Front.

An igneous intrusion, magma or rock born of heat and fire, was squirted upward from within the earth through a fissure, coming to the surface as lava to build this formation. It was most likely formed about 50 million years ago at the time of igneous activity in Central Montana.

Grazing in the shadow of Haystack Butte.

Photo: JEFF VAN TINE

Glaciers and Floods

Massive ice sheets of the continental flow that came from Canada and those sent forth from the mountains played a major role in shaping the physical features of the Front Range and adjacent prairie. The most notable of these frozen rivers passed through the Sun River Canyon and spread out to meet the southern edge of the prairie ice. Proof of the extent of this mountain glacier is a large terminal moraine that sits between Augusta and the canyon's mouth. North of here, many low-lying hills are sprinkled with glacial erratics—rocks not native to the area and brought from elsewhere by the moving ice, in this case Canada. Together, the enormous ice sheets and the glaciers originating in the heights created potholes and wetlands that are important to today's wildlife habitat. The ice from the north advanced and retreated many times over the ages, leaving behind glacial deposits of all shapes and sizes. Indigenous peoples who at one time traveled the Front used some as bison jumps, one of their methods of hunting the shaggy beasts.

More recent natural events redesigned parts of the Rocky Mountain Front. In June 1964, copious amounts of rain dropped on a heavy mountain snowpack, sending an epic tide of water gushing eastward out of the mountains. The destructive flood left extensive scars of disruption on the terrain. Once-vegetated riverbanks and grassy floodplains are now partially barren and littered with boulders, rocks, and gravel that originally were part of the mountains. Foliage is finally beginning to return. The devastation of this flood and another in 1975 is especially evident in the Sun River Canyon, Teton River, and Birch Creek drainages.

Colorful wildflowers, such as prickly pear cactus and fireweed, add a softness to the often harsh landscape.
Photos: RICK and SUSIE GRAETZ

Badger Creek in the northern reaches of the Front.
Photo: JOHN LAMBING

Time and Space

Most geographers agree that physical and historical geography should never be separated. Montana's Rocky Mountain Front offers a textbook example of how time and space need to be studied together to completely understand this riveting place.

Aside from the Great North Trail and its human travelers, the Front Range was home to some of the earliest known wildlife on the planet. Maiasaura, or "Good Mother Lizard," a giant dinosaur found with hatchlings, eggs, and nests was discovered just west of Choteau in an area known as "Egg Mountain." Excavations have since found other, previously unknown kinds of dinosaurs here.

And much later in the annals of the Front, stories of the "Old West" played out in real life. Native Americans, trappers, traders, missionaries, ranchers, cowboys, and the US Military all took on roles in a colorful drama that spanned 50 years and more.

Intense and often hostile interactions among the great Indian Nations who claimed this place and those who entered it reveal accounts unlike any in the nation. At one time, bison roamed here by the hundreds of thousands, making the land fruitful hunting grounds to be fought over. From the mid-18th thru the mid-19th century, the Blackfeet Nation controlled the prairie country in the shadow of the RMF and battled Salish, Kootenai, Gros Ventres, Nez Perce, and other tribes, especially those from west of the Continental Divide who annually "went to buffalo." After the 1860s, though, as the Blackfeet's might weakened and treaties to allow common hunting territory came into play, the hostilities began waning.

By the 1830s, the first white men arrived specifically to trap fur-bearing animals and to trade with various tribes, especially the Blackfeet. By the late 1840s, a decline in demand for furs and the depletion of the beaver ended this profession. Throughout the 1840s and 1850s, missionaries, led by the Jesuits, were active along the Front. Soon, cattlemen, enticed by the nutritious prairie grasses, established many of the ranches that yet exist here today. By 1867, in order to, as they claimed, "control the Blackfeet," the US Military, through the establishment of Fort Shaw, made its presence known. One broken promise after another, land given and land taken away; finally, by the 1880s, the Blackfeet were forced onto the reservation.

Along the length of the Front, ranches and farms have plenty of "breathing room."

Photo: JEFF VAN TINE

Weather

Weather and climate on the Rocky Mountain Front can be as wild as the landscape it affects. Records and extremes are commonplace. Winds, especially those of winter, that roar down from the heights are legendary. Air passing over the Northern Rockies is forced through gaps in the Front's wall, accelerating its speed. Gusts of 133 and even 143 mph have been recorded. And just south of East Glacier, where the air never seems to be still, the average monthly wind speed is almost 25 mph. Of special note are strong Chinooks that can exceed hurricane force of 75 mph at times. Native Americans called these warm winds "snow eaters." Heating up at 5.5 degrees for every thousand feet they descend on the east side of the Sawtooth Range, chinooks can melt or evaporate two feet of snow overnight.

With nothing but open prairie to the north of the RMF, cold arctic air masses, taking leave of the polar regions, rush unimpeded southward and can lower temperatures quickly and dramatically. One day in January of 1916, thanks to a warm chinook wind, Browning was enjoying a balmy 44 degrees; in less than 24 hours, the temperature dropped to 56 degrees below zero. These frigid fronts with rising winds coming from the north and northeast can unload significant amounts of snow at lower elevations.

This event is known as upsloping. In February 1972, on Marias Pass, a low crossing of the Continental Divide and Front Range, one storm brought on by a rising air left 77.5 inches behind before it abated.

A chinook plays out over the crest of the Rocky Mountain Front west of Augusta.

Photo:
RICK and SUSIE GRAETZ

Our Suggestions to You

To understand the infinite value of this majestic piece of our state, probe its roads and trails in all seasons. In the long light of a summer evening, watch as all the details of the heights slowly fade leaving a purple silhouette on the horizon. Catch the intense, color-changing, first light of a rising sun on Castle Reef or Ear Mountain. In autumn, marvel at the delicate gold of the aspens and cottonwoods in the canyons of the Teton River.

On a bright January day, from the high point of the highway between Augusta and Choteau, scan the white immensity of what lies before you. And on a late May or June evening, inhale the intoxicating aroma of wildflowers that blanket the undulating hills.

There are several good locations to access the Front. In the north, from Dupuyer on Hwy 89, a route points west to Swift Reservoir and the North and South forks of Birch Creek, entryways to the Bob Marshall and Great Bear Wilderness areas. Seven miles north of Choteau, also on Hwy 89, a road heads toward the Front. Just before the mountains, the route splits with one following the South Fork of the Teton River and the other leading to the North and West forks. Along the way and at the end of each are great scenic surprises.

On Hwy 287, the town of Augusta provides easy entry into the southern Front. One byway goes west to the Sun River Canyon and Gibson Reservoir and another to Benchmark, a favorite horse route into the "Bob." Hwy 435, extending west and south of Augusta, points to Bean Lake and the Dearborn Canyon.

Much has been penned about the Front, eloquent words all; but in our opinion, the late A.B. "Bud" Guthrie, Jr.'s passion, love and commitment to the landscape he called home spill out in short poetic refrains that resonate a call to action within us. A Pulitzer Prize winner and the originator of the term Big Sky, Bud just might have said it best with this...

"What price, the sight of an antlered head through the pines? What price, the silver shimmer of a trout as it rises to the fly? What price, the sight of a moose in an overgrown pond? How much for a mountain? How much for a glimmer glass lake, for a clear and limitless sky?" —A.B.G., Jr.

Opposite page:

Top: Elk enjoying the safety of the Sun River Game Preserve.

Center: Aspen patterns.

Bottom: Taking the back road home.

This page: Montana's State Flower, the Bitterroot.

All Photos: JEFF VAN TINE

"The Front is unique. Its peril is real. Solutions are hard

to find. To use an old Western expression, I'm reaching

the end of my rope. But I shall never stop caring.

Today I put the job in your fresher, stronger hands.

Fight for the Front, you younger folk. Find the answers."

—A. B. Guthrie, Jr. 1901-1991

SOMETHING SACRED by Gene Sentz

Aldo Leopold spoke of "a sense of place." When one comes to know intimately a special wild place, one feels the sacred there. We touch the earth and are touched by it. We may not own the deed, but we can get very possessive of a place, especially when we become possessed by its extraordinary landscapes.

The Montana Rocky Mountain Front is my special place. From Choteau's Airport Hill, I can see 50 miles northwest across Birch Creek to Feather Woman Mountain. From there southward 75 miles downrange stands Caribou Peak above Falls Creek. Filling the spaces between are Walling Reef and Old-Man-of-the-Hills on Dupuyer Creek; Mount Frazier and Mount Werner in Blackleaf Canyon; Choteau, Baldy, Rocky and Ear mountains feeding the Teton; and Chute Mountain above Deep Creek. Castle Reef and Sawtooth guard the Sun River. Across Ford Creek, Crown Mountain and Steamboat keep watch over the Dearborn, and Scapegoat pierces the distant horizon. And that's only part of it.

The Front was "backbone of the world" to the Blackfeet and other Native Americans and to the ancients who trekked the Old North Trail. The peaks and ridges were vision quest sites. They've been called by different names, but these same mountains remain little changed by millennia. Little more than two centuries ago, no white man had ever seen them, yet now they are sacred in many non-Indian eyes, just as they remain so to the traditionalists of the tribes.

The resilient, slow-growing
limber pine stands tall
against the Northern Lights.

Photo: Dave Hanna

Forest Service evaluations score the public lands along the East Front of the Montana Rockies as the finest unclassified wild country in the lower 48 states. Its scenic splendor is unsurpassed by any undeveloped landscape on earth. Biologists place it in the top one percent of wildlife habitat in North America. The Front is sacred to a growing number of people.

But, as one old-timer who grew up beside the Rockies says, "It's almost like the original temptation. We have this incredibly beautiful place that we can either leave alone or go in and grab the apple." Yes, there are those who wish to build roads and carve mines and drill sites here to prospect for potential resources. Their cry is "Jobs! Revenue! Profits!" I hold no grudge against them, but in this case I agree with the great majority of folks who have said, "Leave the Rocky Mountain Front alone. Save this magnificent landscape in its wild state for future generations. Let it be."

Many people wish to preserve the Front as home for eagles and elk, grizzlies and goats, jack pine and juniper, and other plants and critters, some endangered. Certain economists predict long-term benefits of saving it far outweigh short-term profits to be gained from industrial development. Backcountry recreationists believe too many roads already intrude on public land. And many scientists urge that all remaining wild country be set aside as a baseline from which to compare our mostly developed world.

There are lots of reasons for saving the Front, but the purest I've heard came from a crusty old Montana native who told his congressman, "Some places on earth should be left alone even if solid gold lies beneath them. The Rocky Mountain Front is such a place."

I agree. For me, these special mountains and valleys, in and of themselves, are reason enough. I know them like brothers and sisters and cherished old friends. I keep returning to them. Always, they touch me. I suspect I am possessed by them.

Wallace Stegner described America's remaining wilderness as our "geography of hope." The wild horizons of the Rocky Mountain Front and Bob Marshall Wilderness symbolize the geography of hope for an entire continent. It is an extraordinary land. I trust we can keep it. Something there is sacred.

The Dearborn River.

Photo: CHUCK HANEY

Gene Sentz lives in Choteau, is a retired schoolteacher and a fierce defender of the Front. He has gained an intimate understanding of the area through his many summers working with outfitters in the Bob Marshall Wilderness. This knowledge of the Rocky Mountain Front, and his passion for it, has gained him respect for his opinions with key decision-makers.

Today, Gene spends even more time roaming this landscape, and continues packing and guiding with his outfitter friends.

Small, pleasant,

unobtrusive

communities

are set well to

the east of the

mountains.

TOWNS OF THE FRONT By Rick and Susie Graetz

AUGUSTA

In early July of 1806, Captain Meriwether Lewis, on his way to the Sun River and the falls of the Missouri, wrote in his journals of viewing "Shishequaw Mountain" (Haystack Butte) to the south of present-day Augusta; later in the day he and his men "hunted and dined on Shishequaw Creek (Elk Creek) and as they passed within striking distance of the future town, they "much rejoiced at finding ourselves in the plains of the Missouri which abound with game."

Founded in 1884 by a rancher who named it after his daughter, Augusta has remained historically intact, an excellent example of a small Montana ranching town of a century ago. It might be small (310 residents), but knows how to have a good time. In the cattlemen's tradition, folks here have been hosting the state's oldest, and one of Montana's most popular rodeos for more than three-quarters of a century. Since the late 1940s, recreation has also become an important industry in the area. Fishing, hunting, wilderness pack trips, backpacking and hiking in the nearby Bob Marshall Wilderness have brought new economic development through outfitters, guides and local dude ranches. Entrance to the mountains and the magnificent wild country within is easy, as both the Sun River Canyon Road and the route to the Bob Marshall/Benchmark trailhead lead off from the western edge of town.

Main Street, Augusta.

Photo: RICK and SUSIE GRAETZ

Above: Rocky Mountain Front wetlands.

Photo: TONY BYNUM

Opposite page: Friendly faces are the norm on the Front.

Photo: RICK and SUSIE GRAETZ

BYNUM

Named for early settlers in the area—the Bynum family, in 1881 it was solely a country store. The post office wasn't established until 1885 and the first school in 1899. In 1913, in order to be nearer to the newly built Great Northern railroad from Choteau to Dupuyer, the town picked itself up and relocated a few miles to its present site. A short-lived boom period ensued, but by 1917, the town's population began to decline with the arrival of an extended drought.

Don't be misled by its size (31 people as of 2010). Bynum is home to the Two Medicine Dinosaur Center, a first-class, professional education and research facility. Its star resident is the first infant maiasaura found at the nearby famous Egg Mountain. Roads from Bynum lead toward Muddy Creek and Blackleaf Canyon portions of the Rocky Mountain Front.

PENDROY

Just seven miles north of Bynum and two miles east of Highway 89 sits Pendroy. Named for Levi Boots Pendroy, a Great Northern Railway employee who helped survey the area, the town was started in 1916 as a railroad branch line from Bynum. It grew quickly and was at its most prosperous level in the 1920s. Today, approximately 150 people live in the Pendroy area.

Time out for a fun photo-op in Choteau.

Photo: RICK and SUSIE GRAETZ

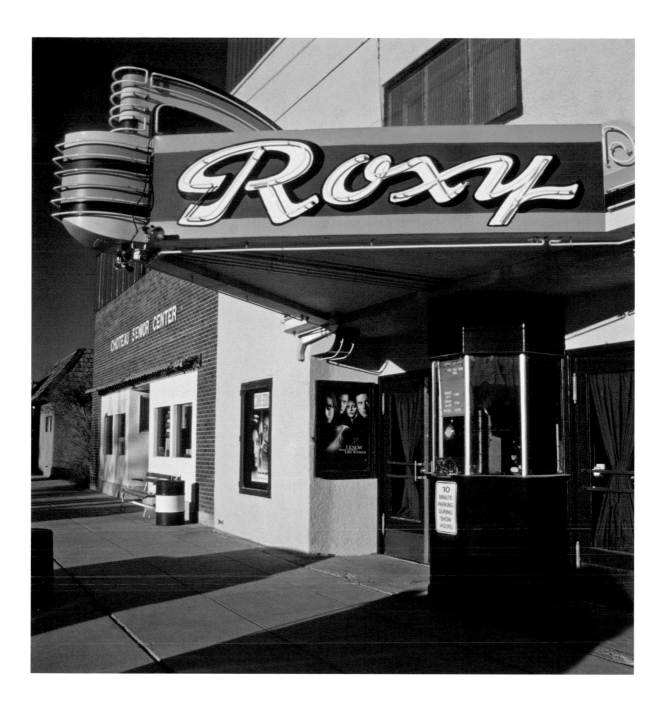

The Roxy Theater has been a colorful
presence in Choteau since 1946.

Photo: RICK and SUSIE GRAETZ

CHOTEAU

The county seat of Teton County is one of the oldest settlements in this part of Montana. When the Blackfeet Indian Agency was relocated north to the reservation boundary in 1876, the few residents left behind eventually moved three miles to the south of the old fort and established the present-day town. In 1883, it was dubbed Choteau after Pierre Chouteau, who was the head of the American Fur Company. The townsfolk preferred to keep the incorrect spelling so as to distinguish their city from Chouteau County.

Today, this agricultural town of 1,684 people is a most attractive community featuring a wide, business-lined main street and a stately stone courthouse that is on the National Register of Historic places. The Old Trail Museum, a complex of historic area buildings and a dinosaur exhibit that conducts educational field study programs in paleontology, gives an entertaining insight into the area's near and far past.

Choteau prides itself as being one of the gateways to the Rocky Mountain Front and the Bob Marshall Wilderness. Within half an hour, you have access to some of the best scenery, horseback riding, hiking, backpacking and backcountry skiing in the Front Range. Until his death in 1991, Pulitzer Prize-winning author A.B. Guthrie, Jr. lived just west of town.

Celebrating July 4th
in Choteau.

Photo: JEFF VAN TINE

FAIRFIELD

Located 12 miles southeast of Choteau, Fairfield sits on a bench overlooking Freezeout Lake with a wide panorama of the Rocky Mountain Front as a backdrop. Fairfield's origins are linked to the Milwaukee Railroad, but irrigation projects in the earliest years of the 20th century allowed for more grain to be grown in the area drawing people to establish homesteads. Platted in 1916 by Elmer Genger, today it is the "Malting Barley Capital of the World" and a trade center for the farming community.

DUPUYER

Originally a stage stop on the bull-team freight route between Fort Benton and Fort Browning, Dupuyer became a supply depot for local ranchers and miners. The post office was established in 1882 and by 1903 the town had grown into a bustling commerce center. Today, this

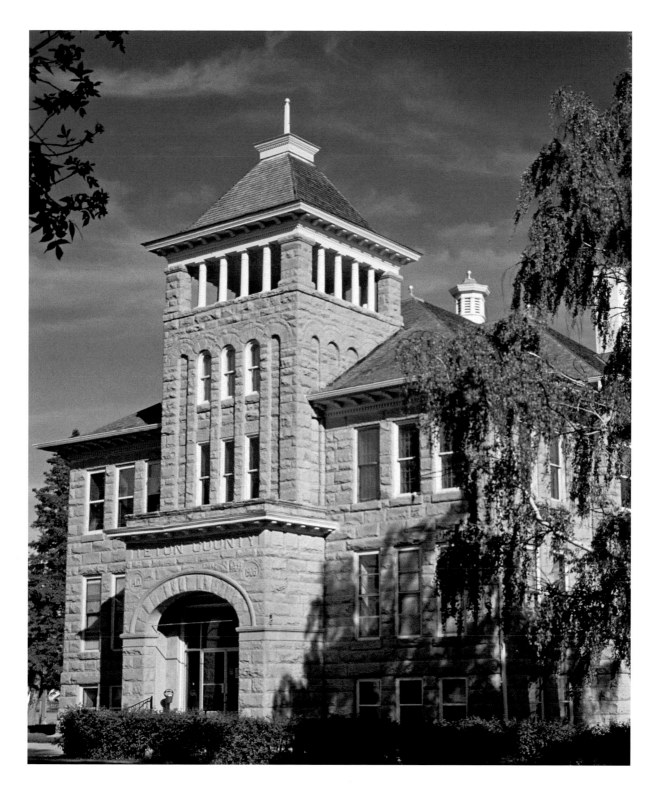

small country hamlet has approximately 86 residents who lead a much quieter lifestyle. Several roads head west toward the northern portions of the Rocky Mountain Front and the trailheads into the Bob Marshall and Great Bear Wilderness Areas. One of them ends at Swift Dam and the Birch Creek trailheads.

Choteau's stately Teton County Courthouse, built in 1906, is on the National Register of Historic Places.

Photo: RICK and SUSIE GRAETZ

HEART BUTTE

Named for nearby mountains that look like inverted hearts and located on the Blackfeet Indian Reservation, Heart Butte is one of the closest towns on the Front to the wall of mountains. The post office was established in 1915, and today approximately 580 people call it home. Situated well off of Hwy 89, Heart Butte can be reached from Dupuyer and from several points farther north.

BROWNING

Named for a US Commissioner of Indian Affairs, Browning is the agency headquarters for the Blackfeet Indian Reservation. Sited at the junction of Hwy 2 and Hwy 89, and only 18 miles from Glacier National Park, it is a tourist stop for gas and snacks and home to about 1,016 full-time residents. There has been a post office here since 1900, but the town wasn't incorporated until 1919. The Blackfeet National Bank, established in 1987, was the first and only tribally controlled, reservation-based, full-service, commercial bank in the United States. Fully accredited since 1985, the Blackfeet Community College provides a means for a better way of life. This busy, mostly Native American town is home to the excellent Museum of the Plains Indians. The Tribal Council is working in conjunction with the Nature Conservancy of Montana to protect reservation lands.

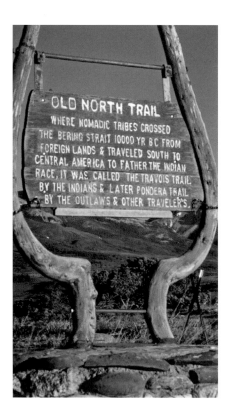

EAST GLACIER

Located on Hwy 2 and serving the southeast entrance to Glacier National Park, East Glacier is the only town along the Front that truly sits hard up against the mountains.

This colorful burg has 363 full-time residents. Most are professionals who work in the Browning schools and hospital or for the National Park Service. During the tourist season the population swells to about 2,500 folks.

Extensive gardens lead from the chalet-style Amtrak train depot to the grand and historic Glacier Park Lodge with its wonderful lobby pillared by enormous four-story-tall Douglas fir logs.

Above: North American Indian Days is held in Browning in early July.

Opposite page: An Old North Trail marker.

Photos: RICK and SUSIE GRAETZ

Sawtooth Reef (center) and
the sweep of the Front.

Photo: RICK and SUSIE GRAETZ

Above: Hiking the Nature Conservancy's Pine Butte Swamp Preserve, which protects one of the grizzly bear's last strongholds on the plains.

Photo: SIMON WILLIAMS/THE NATURE CONSERVANCY

Opposite page:

Rocky Mountain Front ranch.

Photo: RICK and SUSIE GRAETZ

"There is a delight in the hardy life of the open...the nation behaves well if it treats the natural resources as assets which it must turn over to the next generation increased and not impaired in value. Conservation means development as much as it does protection."

—Theodore Roosevelt, 1858-1919 *President of the United States*

A truly amazing ecosystem...

at once peaceful and exciting,

subtle and grand,

wild and settled,

preserved yet endangered.

American bald eagle.

Photo: STEVEN GNAM

Early November, the Front
from a high point between
Augusta and Choteau.

Photo: RICK and SUSIE GRAETZ

Above:

Treasures found on the range.

Photo: RICK and SUSIE GRAETZ

Opposite page:

Cataract Falls gently cascades off

a cliff on Steamboat Mountain.

Photo: WILL KLACZYNSKI

Bulldogging event at the
popular Augusta Rodeo.

Photo: JEFF VAN TINE

Top left: Marmots.   Photo: WILL KLACZYNSKI

Top right: Black-necked stilt.   Photo: JEFF VAN TINE

Bottom: Mountain goat kids.   Photo: WILL KLACZYNSKI

Grizzly bear.

Photo: STEVEN GNAM

Old Man Winter blows
into the Front.

The spine of the Rocky Mountain Front.

Pack mules on winter break.

Photo: RICK and SUSIE GRAETZ

Amtrak rolls off the
Continental Divide out
of East Glacier.

Photo: RICK and SUSIE GRAETZ

"What a country chooses to

save is what a country

chooses to say about itself."

—Mollie H. Beattie, 1947-1996
  Director, U.S. Fish and Wildlife Service

Dinosaur dig with the Two Medicine

Dinosaur Center.

Photo: COURTESY OF TWO MEDICINE

DINOSAUR CENTER

The town of Bynum's "pet dino."

Photo: RICK and SUSIE GRAETZ

The Old Trail Museum in Choteau.

Photo: RICK and SUSIE GRAETZ

The Teton River flows
from the mountains out
into the prairie.

Photo: DOUGLASS DYE

"My father considered a walk among the mountains as the equivalent of churchgoing."

—Aldous Huxley, 1894-1963 *Writer*

Sunday morning hike in God's church.

Photo: RICK and SUSIE GRAETZ

Coffee break with co-workers, ranch-style.

A boy named Beckett and his best friend, Annie.

Photo: RICK and SUSIE GRAETZ

Northern pygmy owl.

There is a spiritual essence to a
Rocky Mountain Front sunrise.

Photo: RICK and SUSIE GRAETZ

"I'm a person of the mountains and the open paddocks and the big empty sky, that's me, and I knew if I spent too long away from all that I'd die; I don't know what of, I just knew I'd die."

—John Marsden *Writer, Educator*

Lake Theboe.

Photo: CHUCK HANEY

Above:

Just like days of the Old West.

Opposite page:

True cowboys start young.

Photos: JEFF VAN TINE

Ear Mountain and spring flowers grace the
Rocky Mountain Front west of Choteau.

Photo: JOHN LAMBING

Three generations of the Grimes family carry on the tradition of backpacking and hiking in the Bob.

Photo: RICK and SUSIE GRATZ

Outfitter Dusty Crary brings a pack string
home after descending Route Creek Pass.

Photo: RICK and SUSIE GRAETZ

A sweep of the RMF and Freezeout Lake Wildlife Management Area brings the lyrics, "And purple mountain majesties above the fruited plain" to mind.

Photo: RICK and SUSIE GRAETZ

Photo: CHUCK HANEY

"The land belongs to the future…that's the way it seems to me. How many names on the county clerk's plat will be there in fifty years? I might as well try to will the sunset over there to my brother's children. We come and go, but the land is always here. And the people who love it and understand it are the people who own it—for a little while."

—Willa Cather 1873-1947 *Writer*

A perfect day on the Rocky Mountain Front

comes to a close.